Prayers before Holy Communion

- Holy Mary, my dearest Mother,
  pray for me
  and make my heart ready
  for Jesus.

- Be with me when He comes.

- Love Him for me.

- Good Saint Joseph,
  pray for me
  that I may love Jesus
  as you loved Him.

- My Guardian Angel,
  help me to be good.

- Jesus, come to me
  because I love You.

This book belongs
to

⋯⋯⋯⋯⋯⋯⋯⋯⋯⋯

⋯⋯⋯⋯⋯⋯⋯⋯⋯⋯

Date ⋯⋯⋯⋯⋯⋯⋯⋯⋯⋯⋯

Presented by

⋯⋯⋯⋯⋯⋯⋯⋯⋯⋯⋯

RECEIVING HOLY COMMUNION

How to Make
A Good Communion

By REV. LOVASIK, S.V.D.

Nihil Obstat: James T. O'Connor, S.T.D., Censor Librorum
Imprimatur: ✠ Patrick J. Sheridan, D.D., Vicar General, Archdiocese of New York

The Nihil Obstat and Imprimatur are official declarations that a book or pamphlet is free of doctrinal or moral error. No implication is contained therein that those who have granted the Nihil Obstat and Imprimatur agree with the contents, opinions or statements expressed.

THE INSTITUTION OF THE
HOLY EUCHARIST

O N the night He was betrayed, Jesus took bread and gave it to His disciples, and said: **"Take this, all of you, and eat it: this is My Body which will be given up for you."**

When supper was ended, He took the cup. Again He gave thanks and praise, gave the cup to His disciples, and said: **"Take this, all of you, and drink from it: this is the cup of My Blood, the Blood of the new and everlasting covenant. It will be shed for you and for all so that sins may be forgiven. Do this in memory of Me."**

Our Lord changed bread and wine into His Body and Blood and offered Himself to God. This was a sacrifice. This was His Body to be offered on the Cross. This was His Blood to be shed for the forgiveness of sins. He told the Apostles that He would die on the next day. That would be the **bloody** sacrifice on the Cross.

Jesus wanted this **unbloody** sacrifice to continue on earth till the end of time. When He told the Apostles to do as He had done, He made them priests with the power to offer this sacrifice.

JESUS OFFERS HIMSELF
IN THE MASS

AFTER our Lord returned to heaven, the Apostles continued to offer this Eucharistic Sacrifice. They ordained other priests. In this way Jesus gave us the priesthood and the Mass.

In the Mass Jesus gives Himself to His Heavenly Father, as He did on the Cross, but now in an unbloody manner in the Sacrament of the Eucharist, for He cannot suffer anymore.

The Sacrifice of the Mass is the same Sacrifice that Jesus offered on the Cross. In every Mass Christ is present, acting through His priest, under the appearances of bread and wine.

In every Mass His Death becomes present, offered as our sacrifice to God in an unbloody and sacramental manner. As often as the Sacrifice of the Cross is celebrated on an altar, the work of our redemption is carried on.

At Mass we offer Christ, our Passover Sacrifice, to God, and we offer ourselves along with Him. We then receive the risen Lord, our Bread of Life, in Holy Communion.

5

6

THE MASS—OUR GREATEST GIFT TO GOD

THE Mass is a true sacrifice because in it Jesus continues His Sacrifice of the Cross, and He gives us the graces He won for us when He died for our salvation.

There is nothing that we can give God as a gift that is greater than His own Son. We offer Jesus to His heavenly Father in the Mass as our Greatest Gift to God.

We join with Jesus and the priest in offering to God this highest form of worship:

1. To give God the highest adoration and glory.
2. To thank Him for all His blessings.
3. To make up for all our sins.
4. To obtain all the blessings we need.

In the Mass it is Jesus Christ, the God-Man, Who is our High Priest and our Victim, praying for us to His heavenly Father.

HOLY COMMUNION HELPS US TO LOVE GOD AND EACH OTHER

HOLY Communion makes sanctifying grace grow in our soul. That grace helps us to love God. That same grace helps us to love our neighbor for the love of God.

Jesus also strengthens us through actual or sacramental grace when we receive Him in Holy Communion. That grace gives light to our mind and strength to our will to do good and to avoid evil. Through Holy Communion we receive the grace to overcome temptation and avoid sinning against God and our neighbor.

Only by the help of this sacramental grace can we truly live in a life of love and fulfill God's greatest commandment: "You shall love the Lord your God with all your heart . . . and your neighbor as yourself" (Matthew 22:37). And our Lord's own commandment: "I give you a new commandment: Love one another " (John 13:34).

The Eucharist is a sacrament of unity because it unites us more closely with God and with one another.

CONDITIONS FOR RECEIVING COMMUNION

To receive Holy Communion you must:

1. Have your soul free from mortal sin.
2. Not eat or drink anything for one hour before Holy Communion. But water may be taken at any time before Holy Communion.

Before Holy Communion you should:

1. Think of Jesus.
2. Say the prayers you have learned.
3. Ask Jesus to come to you.

After Holy Communion you should:

1. Thank Jesus for coming to you.
2. Tell Him how much you love Him.
3. Ask Him to help you.
4. Pray for others.

EXAMINING YOUR CONSCIENCE

In order to be as holy as possible when you receive Communion, ask yourself some questions such as:

- **Did I obey my parents?**
- **Did I always tell the truth?**
- **Did I try to help others?**
- **Did I say my prayers?**
- **Did I fight with anyone?**
- **Did I make fun of anyone?**
- **Did I take anything that does not belong to me?**
- **Did I do my homework and my chores?**

After you have finished asking yourself these and other questions, ask God for forgiveness by saying an ACT OF CONTRITION, such as:

O MY God, I am sorry for all my sins with my whole heart.
I will try to be better in the future.

Sometimes you may wish to go to Confession before receiving Communion.

GETTING READY AT HOME TO RECEIVE COMMUNION

Although we can receive Communion on any day, we usually receive it on Sunday. Sunday is a special day. It is the day set aside for us to give thanks and praise to God, especially by participating in the Holy Mass. On Sunday, we rest from the usual things we do every day and think about God and the things of God.

Sunday is also a special day for the family. We dress in our best clothes and enjoy a family dinner. We may go on a picnic or take a drive or visit our relatives. We should have a special happiness all day and be good to others.

We should also say a special prayer in honor of the Blessed Trinity:

Thank You, GOD THE FATHER.
You made me to know, love, and serve You and to be happy forever in heaven with You.

Thank You, GOD THE SON.
You died and rose from the dead to save me.

Thank You, GOD THE HOLY SPIRIT.
You were sent by the Father and the Son to make me holy.

AT MASS — JOIN IN THE SINGING

At Mass, we think about God. We talk with God. We even sing to God.

So, when you are at Mass, be sure to do the following things:

- Join in the singing to celebrate the wonderful opportunity you have to meet Jesus in this Mass even though you cannot see Him.
- Do everything you can to be united with the priest and people in offering the Mass to God.
- Think of the Father, Who made us.
- Think of Jesus Who died so that we might live forever.
- Think of the Holy Spirit, Who is always giving us His help.
- Think of our Blessed Mother, Mary, who prays for us to her Divine Son Jesus.
- Most of all, be thankful that you can receive Jesus in Communion.

AT MASS — LISTEN TO THE READINGS

At Mass, the Word of God is read to us. God's Word tells us how to live as followers of Jesus.

So, when you are at Mass, be sure to do the following things:

- Listen to the First and Second Readings.
  They come from the Bible.
  They speak of God's love for us
  throughout history
  and especially of God's love
  shown to us in Jesus.

- After the First Reading,
  join in the response that is said or sung
  by everyone.

- When you rise to hear the Gospel,
  remember that the priest or deacon reads it
  in the name of Jesus.
  It is Jesus Himself
  Who becomes present among us
  through His word.

- Then listen to the homily,
  which shows us how to live God's word
  in our lives.

AT MASS — RESPOND TO THE PRAYERS

At Mass, the priest says many prayers. We have special responses to make to some of these prayers.

So, when you are at Mass, be sure to do the following things.

- Make the responses to the prayers.
- Say the proper response when the priest says, "Let us proclaim the mystery of faith."

A Christ has died,
Christ is risen,
Christ will come again.

B Dying you destroyed our death,
rising you restored our life,
Lord Jesus, come in glory.

C When we eat this bread and drink this cup,
we proclaim your death, Lord Jesus,
until you come in glory.

D Lord, by your cross and resurrection
you have set us free.
You are the Savior of the world.

AT MASS — PRAY SILENTLY
BEFORE COMMUNION

Before receiving Communion, the priest prays silently for a few moments. You too can say a silent prayer as final preparation before receiving Jesus in Communion.

JESUS, I believe in You.
Jesus, I hope in You.
Jesus, I love You with all my heart.

Jesus, I want so much to receive You
into my heart.

I long for You.

Jesus, I am sorry for all my sins.

I am not good enough for You to come to me.

But I know You want me to come to You
that You may make me good.

Jesus, give me Your grace
that I may always please You.

Holy Mary, my dearest Mother, pray for me
and make my heart ready for Jesus.

AT MASS — PRAY ALOUD
BEFORE COMMUNION

The priest now invites all to receive Communion.

Say with all the people:

Lord, I am not worthy to receive you,
but only the say the word and I shall be
healed.

The priest then receives Communion.

AT MASS — RECEIVE JESUS
WITH DEVOTION

After the priest receives Communion, it is time for us to receive Jesus. So be sure to do the following:

- **Join the Communion Procession and sing the hymns that tell of your love for Jesus.**

- **Bear in mind that you are going to receive the Body and Blood, Soul and Divinity of the Lord.**

- **Make the proper response when you reach the priest or minister of Communion.**

Priest or other minister: **The Body of Christ.**

- **Answer: Amen.**

- **Receive the Sacred Host on your tongue or in your hand.**

If the Precious Blood is to be received from the Cup, then one again answers Amen when the minister says: "The Blood of Christ."

Priest or other minister: **The Blood of Christ.**

- **Answer: Amen.**

- **Receive the Precious Blood from the Cup.**

AT MASS — THANK JESUS
AFTER COMMUNION

During the Time of Silence that follows Communion, you may say private prayers of thanks to Jesus.

JESUS, I believe in You.
Jesus, I hope in You.
Jesus, I love You with all my heart.
Jesus, I thank You for having come to me.
Welcome to my heart and bless me.

You are the same Jesus
Who loved little children
and let them come to You.

You are the same Jesus
Who gave Your life for us on the Cross
and rose from the dead.

And now that You are so close to me,
I ask You to help me
to love You more
and to serve You as You want me
to serve You.

JESUS IS WITH US IN THE TABERNACLE

Jesus is present under the appearances of the Consecrated Bread and Wine. The Church expresses this presence of Jesus in the Eucharist by preserving the Consecrated Bread in the tabernacle that is found in every Catholic church.

JESUS, I thank You
    for staying in the tabernacle
    day and night to be with me
    and to hear my prayers
    when I need Your help.

You are my best Friend.

I want to come to visit You often.

I want to show You how much I love You,
    and to ask You to help me
    and those I love.

                    *   *   *

O Sacrament most holy,
    O Sacrament divine!

All praise and all thanksgiving
    be every moment Thine!

PRAYERS TO OUR LADY
OF THE BLESSED SACRAMENT

Since Mary is the Mother of Jesus, she is also known as Our Lady of the Blessed Sacrament. It is good for us to pray to her from time to time.

O VIRGIN Mary,
   we pray to you
   as our Lady of the Blessed Sacrament.

You are the glory of the Christian people,
   the joy of the Universal Church,
   and the salvation of the whole world.

Pray for us,
   and awaken in all believers a deep devotion
   for the most Holy Eucharist.

In this way,
   they may be worthy to receive often
   this holy Sacrament of the Altar.

JESUS IS "GOD WITH US"

WE should adore, love, and thank Jesus in the Blessed Sacrament by our visits to the tabernacle in our churches and in Benediction. Benediction is a ceremony in which the Blessed Sacrament is exposed to the people for adoration. It ends with the priest blessing the people with the Consecrated Bread.

God is really with us in the Mass, in Holy Communion, and in the tabernacle.

Other Great Books for Children

FIRST MASS BOOK—Ideal Children's Mass Book with all the official Mass prayers. Colored illustrations of the Mass and the Life of Christ. Confession and Communion Prayers.   Ask for No. 808

The **STORY OF JESUS**—By Father Lovasik, S.V.D. A large-format book with magnificent full colored pictures for young readers to enjoy and learn about the life of Jesus. Each story is told in simple and direct words.   Ask for No. 535

CATHOLIC PICTURE BIBLE—By Rev. L. Lovasik, S.V.D. Thrilling, inspiring and educational for all ages. Over 110 Bible stories retold in simple words, and illustrated in full color.   Ask for No. 435

LIVES OF THE SAINTS—New Revised Edition. Short life of a Saint and prayer for every day of the year. Over 50 illustrations. Ideal for daily meditation and private study.   Ask for No. 870

PICTURE BOOK OF SAINTS—By Rev. L. Lovasik, S.V.D. Illustrated lives of the Saints in full color. It clearly depicts the lives of over 100 popular Saints in word and picture.   Ask for No. 235

Saint Joseph CHILDREN'S MISSAL—This new beautiful Children's Missal, illustrated throughout in full color. Includes official Responses by the people. An ideal gift for First Holy Communion.   Ask for No. 806

St. Joseph FIRST CHILDREN'S BIBLE—By Father Lovasik, S.V.D. Over 50 of the best-loved stories of the Bible retold for children. Each story is written in clear and simple language and illustrated by an attractive and superbly inspiring illustration. A perfect book for introducing very young children to the Bible.   Ask for No. 135

WHEREVER CATHOLIC BOOKS ARE SOLD

Prayers after Holy Communion

- Jesus, I believe in You.

- Jesus, I hope in You.

- Jesus, I love You.

- Jesus, I thank You
  for having come to me.

- Welcome to my heart
  and bless me.

- You are the same Jesus
  Who gave Your life for us
  on the cross
  and rose from the dead.

- And now You have come
    to me.
  Jesus, I thank You
  for Your love for me.